WHAT IT MEANs TO BE "BORN from Above" John 3:3

By

Rev. Robert L. Whiteley

Copyright © 2011 by Rev. Robert L. Whiteley

What it Means to be Born from Above
John 3:3
by Rev. Robert L. Whiteley

Printed in the United States of America

ISBN 9781613796177

All rights reserved solely by the author. The author guarantees all contents are original and do not infringe upon the legal rights of any other person or work. No part of this book may be reproduced in any form without the permission of the author. The views expressed in this book are not necessarily those of the publisher.

Unless otherwise indicated, Bible quotations are taken from the Revised Standard Version. Copyright © 1962 by The World Publishing Company.

www.xulonpress.com

DEDICATION

This work is dedicated to the ongoing ministry of our Lord, Jesus the Christ.

IN GRATITUDE

I thank my good friend Gerry Lamothe, a former professor of Theology, who sparked my undertaking of this book in one of his classes. He suggested a paper on the Holy Spirit, and has devoted time for review and suggestions as the book developed from that paper. Another person to whom I am deeply indebted is Dr. William Barr, a retired professor of Theology from Lexington Theological Seminary. He, too, patiently reviewed, corrected and suggested clarifications and important viewpoints. Some lay leaders who provided feedback were Valerie Smith and Susan Williams. This witness was made possible with the assistance of my wife, Beverly. She patiently typed and retyped, deciphered my poor handwriting, corrected spelling, restructured sentences, and made suggestions so that readers could more clearly understand the meaning of this witness.

TABLE OF CONTENTS

Introduction	xiii
Born from Above	15
The Old Testament as the Launch Pad	17
A Nighttime Conversation	22
Back to the Beginning	24
A Physical Analogy	26
Rising to the Level of Spirit	28
God's Original Creativity	30
New Life	31
God's Instruction	34
We Are Accountable	36
The Beginning of Sacrifice	41
The Withdrawal of God's Spirit	43
The Divine/Human Relationship	45
God's Providential Guidance	48

TABLE OF CONTENTS (CONTINUED)

The Exodus 50

God's Rebellious People 53

Rules of Life 54

A House for God 57

The Day of Atonement 61

God's Protection and Deliverance 67

Jesus – The Embodiment of God 69

Jesus Endowed with the Spirit 73

A New Covenant 75

A Gift of the Spirit 77

Empowerment by the Spirit 83

Instantaneous or Gradual Rebirth? 85

Walking with the Spirit 86

Conclusion 97

The dying to the old life and rising to a new life.

INTRODUCTION

In an adult Sunday school class I asked the question, "When did the Holy Spirit begin His work?" Each person present answered, "At Pentecost!" That answer seemed to be the prevalent answer among Christians. That answer didn't sit right with me. In my study of who, what, and where of the Holy Spirit, the "when" was left out. In my ministerial occupation, I became more aware of how powerful was the work of the Holy Spirit. After attending college and seminary, where the study of the Holy Spirit was essentially omitted, I felt I missed a vital part of my understanding of God and His love and care of His creation.

I participated in the baptism of many people who had confessed their belief in Jesus the Christ as the Son of God. They expressed their desire to enter into a newness of life. For the most part, I saw very little change in those lives. This observation led me to wonder if baptism was an initiation into a church community rather than an act in response to Jesus' requirement for eternal life. Then the question came to mind as to why Jesus said baptism was required. As I pursued the question, "Why did Jesus say to Nicodemus that he had to be born from above?" no one could tell me why. Again, I was led to research the reason Jesus stated that requirement to Nicodemus. The result of that research is this book.

BORN FROM ABOVE
John 3:3

Lee was a few months old, living in a bassinet, perched in the middle of the front pew of the Community Church – this was Lee's first exposure to what was to become a seventy-year adventure with the Holy Spirit's leading. The odd part of this journey with the Holy Spirit was that for most of the journey, Lee was not aware of the Holy Spirit's leading the way. In fact, the Holy Spirit was not even a conscious factor in his quest to be a minister of the Gospel.

It was not until the early part of Lee's fourth pastorate that the awareness of the leadership and empowerment of the spirit suddenly came upon him. It came when an itinerant, self-proclaimed missionary passed through town, who himself had the guidance and life-saving experience of the Holy Spirit. The missionary said that to deeply understand the work of the Holy Spirit you must go back to the beginning – that is, the first chapter of Genesis.

At that same time, Lee was taking an Old Testament class at a local university and completion of the class required a research paper. Lee's topic was the origin, leadership and empowerment of the Holy Spirit as the foundation for the

Christian faith. Research on this led Lee to realize what Christians have often missed. What Christians must realize is that to understand the New Testament, one must understand the Old Testament, and how the leadership, empowerment and indwelling of God's Spirit works.

This is especially true in order to fully understand Jesus' statement to Nicodemus when Jesus said, "You must be born from above.

THE OLD TESTAMENT AS THE LAUNCH PAD

Many readers of the New Testament do not realize that what was said and done in the New Testament is based on or the result of what was said or done in the Old Testament. More profoundly, the continuity running through the great diversity of God's saving words and actions described in both Testaments is often overlooked.

For example, to understand why Jesus said to Nicodemus (a Pharisee) in John 3:3, that he had to be "born from above" ("Born Anew"), we need to look back to the Old Testament to see why a new birth is necessary and that it was God's will from the beginning (cf. Eph. 1:3-4).

The word used for *born from above* in Greek is *anothen*. William Barclay, in his commentary, defines the Greek word *anothen*, citing three different meanings: (1) it can mean *from the beginning, completely radically;* (2) it can mean *again,* in the sense of *for the second time;* or (3) it can mean *from above,* and therefore, *from God.*

Barclay goes on to say that there is no single word in the English language that encompasses these three meanings. The King James Version translates it as *Born Again*;

the Revised Standard Version translates it as *Born Anew*; the New English Bible translates it as *Born Over Again*. It seems to bring out the larger meaning of Jesus' life and message to translate *anothen* as Barclay's definition *Born from Above* or even better, *Born from God*. The appropriateness of his translation will become clearer as we trace the actions of God through the Old and New Testaments, since these provide the context of Jesus' statement to Nicodemus.

The rebirth from God is essential to experience eternal life in the presence of God for as Jesus said, "Unless one is born anew, he cannot see the Kingdom of God." [John 3:3 RSV] Prior to Jesus' answer, as recorded history has shown, the human race in various ways envisioned and tried in many ways to prepare for an afterlife, from Egyptian mummification to Indian Vedas. Weapons for defense, boats to sail in, gold and silver to buy whatever was needed, even food to eat, were often buried with the deceased. All of this is evidenced in ancient burial chambers in Egyptian and other ancient civilizations. The tomb of King Tutankhamen is a prime example of that ancient practice. In his burial chamber were highly valuable gold and jewels, food, a boat and many items for the afterlife, for the deceased needed all these items for the good afterlife.

To this day, in other religious beliefs, the afterlife depends on performance and wealth. The idea that good deeds take precedence over and against bad deeds is also prevalent. The question that is always in the minds of those who hold this belief is, "Are my good deeds outnumbering my bad deeds?" "Have I gathered enough good deeds to be included in the afterlife and in the presence of God?" Unfortunately, the worshiper is never sure.

On the other hand, for the Christian who confesses belief in Jesus as the Christ, accepts Him as his or her personal Savior and the Son of God who is the Creator and Giver of Life, and is baptized signifying his or her complete willingness to die to an old life and rise to "walk in newness of life" [Romans 6:46], eternal life with God is assured (cf. Romans 6:5–11). Baptism is participation in the death and resurrection of Christ (II Cor. 5:14-15; dv. Gal. 2: 19-20). Once we hear this good news and the Holy Spirit enters the worshiper's life, "good deeds" become a response to God's grace rather than a prerequisite. Paul's use of the word, "walk" means to move forward, not stand still, saying "I have done all I need to do for eternal life." Dr. Wayne Dyer, in his book *Inspiration,* wrote, "Being in Spirit is a direction we take, rather than a destination to be reached. Living our life in-

Spirit requires us to determine that direction, and we do so by noticing our thoughts and behaviors."

Marian fell ill, and since she was the one who did all the meal preparation in her home, her husband was at a loss. They were faithful supporters of the local church, so that prompted the members of the church to step in to help. Each day for weeks, someone showed up with a meal for both Marian and her husband. Marian recovered and the couple was so grateful that they wanted to respond to the love and generosity of their church family. However, they could not, for there were so many to thank.

Marian and her husband did not earn the generosity and love from their congregation's members. It is the same with God's love and generosity. It was and still is a free gift, we do not earn it. We do not earn it even if we could, as you will see as you read on.

Marian and her husband wanted to respond by doing something, showing a deep sense of gratitude. But, what? Could they bake a pie and give each one who came to their rescue a pie with a card saying, "Thank you!" Those who helped were not helping so that they could receive a pie and a thank-you note. They did it as Christians serving others in need. For Marian and her husband to express a deep sense of gratitude was to reach out to others who are in need – in need of love, and maybe a pie would sweeten a bad day.

Gratitude is a response, not a prerequisite to a good deed given to us. So how do we develop a deep sense of gratitude for what God has so graciously given to us through his Son, Jesus the Christ? It is realizing we are helpless, and in need, allowing His Holy Spirit to enter us, healing us and guiding us into a life changing experience. Our response of deep gratitude is to share our experience of God's love with everyone we meet, maybe not in words but perhaps giving them a pie. Our service is one way of saying, "Thank you." Service is the action of a grateful heart.

A NIGHTTIME CONVERSATION

To gain a better understanding of what Jesus said to Nicodemus regarding this new life, let us review the words. " . . . Truly, truly I say to you, unless one is born anew [or from above, or from God] he cannot see the Kingdom of God." [John 3:3] Nicodemus responded by saying, "How can a man be born when he is old? Can he enter a second time into his mother's womb and be born?" It is obvious Nicodemus defined the word *anothen* as *again* or *for the second time* physically. But Jesus was meaning another definition, for Jesus said, "Truly, truly, I say to you, unless one is born of water and the Spirit, he cannot enter the Kingdom of God."

Nicodemus's response is surprising because being reborn was not foreign to the Jews at that time. When someone from another religion wanted to become a Jew and to be accepted into Judaism he had to be cleansed. This cleansing was accomplished by prayer, sacrifice and baptism. It was then that Judaism regarded this man as having been reborn, even though not having a Jewish mother. And, as at Qumran, ritual baptisms of purification were performed. In any case, as John the Baptizer's practice of baptism clearly shows, baptism of repentance was also known to those acquainted with Jesus.

It is this principle of baptism as the beginning of a new life that Jesus is eluding to when he says, "born of water and the Spirit." Water is a cleansing agent, washing away a part of life, dying to an old way of living. The act of washing away leaves a cleansed soul, allowing room for a new life that only the Holy Spirit can fill.

What Jesus taught in this regard is that God, through Jesus the Christ, is reestablishing His relationship that He intended at the beginning – a relationship in which God is the sole bearer and giver of life, and which humans are the grateful recipients of life. Such gratitude is communicated by living life in thanksgiving and service to God.

BACK TO THE BEGINNING

To make this clear, we must return to the beginning as it is recorded in Genesis: *"Beneshit barah Elochim eht hashamayim vaeht haerstz"* [Genesis 1:1 as it appears in the Hebrew text]. In the beginning God created *"eht"* (*aleph/tahr*) the heavens and the earth. *"Eht"*, which is pronounced "eight", is the Hebrew word representing the first and last letters in the Hebrew alphabet. This corresponds to the Greek *Alpha* and *Omega*, and in English, A and Z. *Eht* is considered by the rabbinic scholars as "the word of creation." In Revelation 1:8 we read that God said, "I am the Alpha and the Omega . . . who was and who is to come, the Almighty," giving us sustenance via the Holy Spirit [Genesis 2:7].

The purpose of this book is to trace God's Holy Spirit as it relates to the "Word of Creation" Jesus – how God through the Word (logos) and God's Holy Spirit (the power) relates to humankind's body and spirit and its rebirth.

In Genesis 1:2 we read, "The earth was without form and void, and darkness was upon the face of the deep, and the *Ruach* (Spirit) of God was moving over the face of the waters." Then God spoke, "Let there be firmament . . . Let there be waters . . ." This was the active Logos empowered by the Holy Spirit, the active creative power of God. Since this creative action is also a creating of the creature out of nothingness or the void, it has redemptive significance. This Holy Spirit is the same Holy Spirit that later guided and protected the Hebrew nation to victory over their enemies, the same power given little David as he faced Goliath. It is the same power that was withdrawn from the Hebrew army when they became arrogant and prideful, leaving them fearful, even defenseless. It was the power bestowed on the prophets standing in the face of their enemies, and the same power given to Jesus at His baptism in the form of a dove. The same power that was given to the disciples at Pentecost is ours when we invite the Holy Spirit into our lives. All of creation was spoken into existence through the Word, except humankind. Genesis 1:26 records, "Let us make man in our image, after our likeness . . . ." The immediate questions here are, "Who are 'us'?" and "What is God's image?"

A PHYSICAL ANALOGY

An analogy used to describe "us" is, when we picture God as water, ever flowing water. Frozen water makes a physical solid, in this case, Jesus. Water can be heated to make steam. Steam in a controlled environment creates power. All is water, but in three different forms. The early church theologians used other analogies: sun, rays, beams; river, brook, stream; tree, branches, leaves/blossoms.

But God is not a physical being, because being physical limits movement, but God does have physical manifestations evidenced in human beings as well as in His Son, Jesus the Christ, God incarnate. God as Spirit is a living force, a living energy that is beyond our ability to understand or comprehend. This then leads us to conclude that God is a limitless Spirit energy, but concentrated in persons and relationships. The question of how to understand this more precisely has been a problem from the beginning of interpretation of scripture. Since we live in a physical world, from the beginning, our thinking and ideas were made real primarily in physical terms. Therefore, we find all kinds of images that represent God in this way. It also translates into our idea of what God created, those living things and mankind are to be both physical and spiritual (the "us" suggests spiritual as well as physical relationship).

The result of this idea is that God is pictured as a solitary, unmoved and unmoving "frozen" God with a long grey beard and long flowing robes.

RISING TO THE LEVEL OF SPIRIT

When we read John 4:24, we get a different picture. John emphasizes that "God is Spirit." God is not a physical being, but a living energy force, a universal living limitless energy capable of taking on physical manifestations: face, hands, feet, and above all, as evidenced in God's Son, Jesus [John 1:14]. A God who is capable of creating a universe (sun, stars, earth) is also capable of introducing Himself in the ultimate form of a particular human being.

This leads to the conclusion that God, "Spirit," created man in God's image which is both "body and spirit." [John 4:24] We are an "embodied spirit." Our body is a suitcase, as it were, that contains who we really are, our spirit. It is this "embodied spirit" (in-spiration) that never dies and is intended to return to God who created it in the beginning.

To illustrate this point, Genesis 2:5 states, ". . . and there was no man to till the ground." If God created man physically in Chapter One, there would have been a physical man to till the ground. So, to have someone capable of responsively tilling the ground, God then, ". . . forms man of the dust from the ground, and in breathing (the call to stewardship of the earth which is both spiritual as well as physical) into his nostrils the breath of life . . ." God created humankind spiritually (Gen 1:26) and now He gives humankind a vessel to live and move around in, to till the ground. (The Greek translation of the Hebrew is "*psychen zosan*", a soul having life.) God creates the essence of life only once. Thereafter, God forms life in its manifold varieties. It is through us human beings, who cannot create as God creates, but only discover and modify and extinguish (extinct species some of which we have caused) what has already been created, and then remold it. This is how God allows us to participate in His ongoing creation.

GOD'S ORIGINAL CREATIVITY

It may be in order to define "create" at this point so that we are on the same page. To create is to make from nothing, to originate, to call into being. The word "create" is often misused. God is the only One who is capable of creating. God is the only One who is capable of creating *ex nihilo*, out of nothing (even if, as Dorothy Sayres suggests in *The Mind of the Maker*, creative imagination is a close analogy). All that humans can do, even in inventive or creative thinking, is to combine that which is already created to form a new, previously unknown item. It is in this activity that God's Spirit-energy within the human mind allows us to share in the realm of God's ongoing creation.

NEW LIFE

Spring had arrived and the dormant trees and flowers were beginning to arrive in the newness of life. At 3:30 in the afternoon the announcement came: "It's a boy!!" How fitting, nature coming alive, and a new addition to the human family arrived – kicking and screaming.

At that point, anyone who is aware of the gift of life realizes that this honor and privilege of bringing new life into existence is the only place that the God of creation allows us to join Him, in the truest sense, in His creation. Everything else that we do is either discovery or remolding of what already exists.

It has been thought by others that the two creation stories in Genesis were just that, two versions of the creation. However, this author believes that the stories are two phases of God's ongoing creation as we know it. God's creation was then and still is in stages. It is still evolving as we discover through research how life develops.

Science has through carbon dating and other means now calculated that the universe and the creation of Earth is some two billion years old. They estimate that humans have been around for hundreds of thousands of years, having first appeared in Africa or China. Creation is the "original blessing." When we do not accept this as a blessing, we refute this blessing. Is that refusal the "original sin?"

It is interesting to note that all of what science has discovered to this day and time has always been here and possible to discover. Transplant of vital organs has always been possible, but humankind had not developed enough tools or skills to do what seemed impossible. Stem cells have been forming from the beginning in our entire bodies. Only now are we understanding the function of stem cells and just learning to use those cells to grow replacement parts. Such discoveries are being revealed as we advance the capability to understand and use God's creation.

This does not contradict the Genesis creation story, but only lengthens what was considered to be a day, or a long time. [cf. Ps. 90:4] What is a day for God? This depends on your point of view. From the sun, day never ends; from the view opposite the sun, night never ends. This author is led to believe that through God's ongoing development of His creation God revealed Himself as being the Creator and Sustainer of Life at the point where the human development was capable of receiving, recognizing, and comprehending it, day never ends. [See Ps. 8 and Job 38-40].

Enter Adam and Eve. It is at this point that God's Spirit, now identified, "walked with" the spirit of Adam and Eve. It was God's Spirit that hovered over the Creation, implementing His word (logos). It is the same Spirit that now walked with Adam and Eve guiding them into what to do and what not to do, calling them to exercise free will and to be obedient in faithfulness to God. Adam and Eve through unfaithfulness became aware of obedience and disobedience, of accepting the Spirit of God or choosing to do what they wanted to do, rejecting God's guidance. This is how this author sees God's beginning a direct involvement in our lives, directing His creation and forming civilization. His involvement was to establish rules, to show the way of life for humankind to follow, to be obedient in love and respect, both in reaction to God and in relation to our fellow sojourners on Earth. These dos and don'ts provide the norm for measuring good and bad deeds alluded to earlier.

GOD'S INSTRUCTION

The revelation of God as Creator and God's Spirit who walked with Adam and Eve took place in a "Garden" that God had prepared for them. It is in the garden that He began to teach and guide. ". . . and the Lord God commanded the man, saying, 'You may freely eat of every tree of the garden; but of the tree of knowledge of good and evil, you shall not eat, for the day that you eat of it, you shall die.'" [Genesis 2:17]

True to form of all humans, tell them not to do something and that is exactly what they will do. Eve ". . . took of its fruit (the tree of life) and ate; and she also gave some to her husband, and he ate." [Genesis 3:6] This act constituted the first disobedience, or "sin." Sin, more deeply, was turning away from God and pondering the eating or not eating as a choice by Eve as well as ours. The consequence of this disobedience (sin) was not fully understood until God returns, as we read in the verses 8-11 of Chapter 3. God caught the two in their disobedience. That act constituted the first and basic disobedience, of turning away from God's directive, exercising their free will, making the decision to eat or not to eat. They ate.

John was from a privileged family. Money was plentiful, so he paid cash for most of the items he wanted. At a retail store, John bought a new watch. As usual, he handed the clerk a large denomination of cash, more than enough to pay for the watch. The clerk rang up the cost of the watch, then removed the difference from the drawer and handed John the change. John realized the clerk had handed him more than she should have. He was immediately faced with the question, "Should I tell the clerk of the error, or should I just keep it:" Choices! The words, "Thou shall not steal" ran through John's mind. But, he thought, the store will not miss the money. On the other hand, the clerk will – it may even cost her a job. What happens at the store is not the point. The point is what happens at judgment time – obedience or disobedience.

WE ARE ACCOUNTABLE

This then, calls for accountability on the part of Adam and Eve. The question is posed by God: ". . . Have you eaten of the tree of which I commanded you not to eat?" [Genesis 3:11] Again, true to form, Adam evades accountability and blames Eve, who in turn evades accountability and blames a serpent. It was the first example of "passing the buck" – someone else made me do it – it's not my fault! It seems that from the beginning, no one wanted to accept responsibility for his or her own disobedience.

John called the error to the clerk's attention, saying, "Do you want to give me this amount of money?" The clerk recounted the money, discovered her error and gave John the correct change. Accountability – John could have kept the money and when asked about it later could have said, "It's not my fault. She gave me the wrong change –it's not my fault!" knowing all along the error that had been made.

In the case of Adam and Eve, what made matters worse, and what made God very upset, was that Adam blamed God for his disobedience, for Adam said, "It was the woman you gave me . . . . She gave me the fruit." In essence, Adam said:

If you, (God) had not given me this woman, I would not have disobeyed; it's entirely your fault.

The thought comes to mind that today things would be much different if Adam had not eaten and had counseled Eve to turn back to God and confess that the fruit looked so good she could not resist. God at that time may have bestowed His first act of forgiveness. But Adam did not own up, nor did Eve; and because they more or less blamed God for this misdeed, God became angry.

At that point, God passed judgment on the two. [Genesis 3:16-19] God could have killed them for eating of the tree because God had warned them, "For in the day that you eat of it, you shall die." [Genesis 2:17] To die in this instance may be assumed to be a physical death. What may be more accurately rendered here is that the personal relationship, the intimate Holy Spirit, walking with them and guiding them, dies or is withdrawn, but God by loving His creation, does not shut the door. God still desires a personal relationship, no matter how horrendous the sin. The death that God speaks of is the withdrawal of His spirit, and this becomes the basis for being Born from Above, the reuniting of God's spirit with humankind's spirit.

John learned early on that even living a privileged life, there were "do's" and "don'ts." Do's resulted in rewards, but don'ts resulted in punishment. When John did a "don't" it resulted in a period of reflection, not unlike Dennis the Menace sitting in a corner. It is in this reflection that John learned by owning up to the misdeed he was forgiven. Forgiveness, then, resulted in peace of mind and joy. John also experienced anxiety, fear and discomfort when he did not acknowledge the fault, as he harbored it in his heart. It is in the awareness of do's and don'ts that we discover the relentless pursuit of parents, and especially of God, for us to be honest and accountable, resulting in their forgiveness and validates their love.

What it Means to be Born from Above

Adam and Eve are ejected from the Garden of Eden. They walk alone in darkness, the animal skins provided by God symbolizing the covering over of their sin of disobedience, as the first sacrifice for sin.

God desires that personal, one-on-one relationship. So God grants Adam and Eve a "reprieve," a covering over of their sin. Signifying this grace, God brought them covering for their naked bodies that eating of the tree of knowledge revealed to them: ". . . and the Lord God brought them covering for their naked bodies . . .and the Lord God made for Adam and his wife garments of skins, and clothed them." [Genesis 3:21]

THE BEGINNING OF SACRIFICE

It stands to reason that in order for God to obtain skins to cover Adam and Eve's naked bodies, God had to kill an animal. It then can be said, that killing of an animal was the first sacrifice God made for mankind's sin, right at the beginning of sin by man. This foreshadows the fact that God makes the last sacrifice, the forgiveness of man's sin by giving up His Son, our Lord Jesus the Christ.

God did that last sacrifice because from Adam and Eve to the coming of Jesus, mankind had not and was not capable of atoning for his or her sin. This is true even though Israel celebrated a Day of Atonement (*Yom Kippur*) [see Lev. 16]. Sacrifice to God by the Hebrew people was a reminder to the Hebrews of God's reprieve for sin.

The result of Adam's and Eve's disobedience had a greater impact on them. Other than what is described in Verses 16-19, now God sent the two out of the garden, ". . . therefore, the Lord God sent him [Adam] from the garden [from the nearness to God, Spirit to spirit], to till the ground from which he was taken. He drove out the man; and at the east of the Garden of Eden, He placed the cherubim and a flaming sword which turned every way, to guard the way to the tree of life." [Genesis 3:23].

THE WITHDRAWAL OF GOD'S SPIRIT

The act of God which drove Adam and Eve from the garden, where God's Spirit walked with their spirits, announced the withdrawal of God's guiding Spirit from Adam and Eve's spirits. But because of God's desire and love for His creation, God still remained hovering over them maintaining the breath and the spirit which gives and sustains their lives. At the same time God allowed Adam and Eve's spirits to be free to choose the path they and all who follow would travel.

Ron was in his late teens, traveling with some friends to a neighboring city. Once there, they were involved in a sting operation by the local law enforcement officers. The result was the boys were arrested and put in jail. The call came to his parents, "I'm in jail!" His father drove to the nearby city asking himself all along the way, "Where did I go wrong? What could I have done differently? Is this my fault?" These questions are the result of a deep and abiding love for his son. Otherwise, there would not have been any questions, only, "Stay there! You deserve it!" It was the love of his parents that sustained Ron through the resulting trial.

The withdrawal of God's Spirit left Adam and Eve and the humanity that followed without the power of God's Spirit to withstand the physical and spiritual demands on them, resulting in the flourishing of sin. Man's spirit, in effect, was darkened and leaderless. At that point, man's spirit turned to the only thing it knew, the body and its appetites. There was nowhere else to go. Through all that turmoil, God's love for His creation remained over them even though they were unaware of it.

THE DIVINE/HUMAN RELATIONSHIP

In Genesis 2:7, "God breathed into his nostrils the breath of life," (*ruach*) we read that Adam now had the God's Spirit with him, giving him power. Having had that power of God's Spirit, and now withdrawn as a personal guide, they and all those who follow were left trying but failing to regain that close relationship with God, until we read in John 20:22, "Jesus breathed on them and said to them, 'Receive the Holy Spirit.'" Humankind, through Jesus the Christ was given the gift of the presence and the guiding power of God's Holy Spirit – was opened up to receive and live in God's Spirit. (See the incisive discussion of this in N.T. Wright's *The Challenge of Easter*.)

In the period between Adam's and Eve's expulsion from the garden to the advent of God's Son Jesus, an examination needs to be made as to why Jesus, the Word (logos), had to come and restore the "God-man relationship."

That turning of man's spirit from God's Spirit to man's appetites has caused more and more disobedience and schisms between God and man. This deterioration of God-man relationship got to a point that God said, "I am ... sorry that I had made man on the earth," and it grieved Him.

So the Lord said, 'I will blot out man whom I created from the face of the ground, man and beast and creeping things, and birds of the air, for I am sorry that I have made them'." [Genesis 6:6-7]

However, God, being a patient and persistent loving God, still desiring reconciliation with His creation, once again gives humanity a reprieve. God finds a new heart and devout spirit in a man named Noah. ". . . But Noah found favor in the eyes of the Lord." [Genesis 67:9] Noah was instructed to build an ark, and at the ripe old age of 600 years, Noah, with his wife, sons and their wives, were saved from a flood along with pairs of animals that were to repopulate the earth.

The great flood was a second attempt of God to establish a God-human relationship, the guiding Spirit of God with the spirit of humans and a second attempt to cover over humanity's sin and to make a new covenant of God with man. Noah, in a sense, is another Adam. God starts over, and says, "Behold, I establish my covenant with you and your descendants after you . . . ." [Gen. 9:9] It is interesting to note that the name *Noah* means, the *good-man*. It has been said, "*Adam* means *first-man*, *Noah* means *good-man or godly man*, and *Jesus* means *God-man*. It is in covenant with Noah that God continued to hover over, guiding and protecting the descendents of Noah that God later selects as His "Chosen People." In spite of mankind's inability to adequately atone for their continued disobedience, God's Spirit remained as a guide and protector of His chosen people, the Hebrews, who as a nation were to proclaim to the world who God was and is the giver, sustainer and renewer of life. To accomplish this, God's Spirit walked with a select few for the purpose of proclaiming God's intentions, prophecy, and protection as a witness and blessing to all peoples [Gen. 12:3]

GOD'S PROVIDENTIAL GUIDANCE

Those select few, whom the Holy Spirit was to enter and to guide, essentially began with Abram (later to be renamed by God as *Abraham*). It was Abram's obedience to the guidance of the Holy Spirit to the point of sacrificing his own son, Isaac, that God gave Abram this statement: "I will bless those who bless you, and him who curses you, I will curse; and by you all families of earth shall bless themselves." [Gen. 12:8] God told Abram, who had reached the age of 99, "I am God Almighty; walk before me and be blameless. And I will multiply you exceedingly." [Gen. 17:16] It is at that point that God renamed Abram to be Abraham. He, God, who gives and sustains life, followed that by saying, ". . . for I have made you the father of a multitude of nations. I will make you exceedingly fruitful; and I will make nations of you and kings shall come forth from you. And I will establish my covenant between me and you and your descendants after you throughout their generations for an everlasting covenant, to be God to you and to your descendants after you. And I will give to you and to your descendants after you, the land of your sojourning, all the land of Canaan, for an everlasting possession; and I will be their God." [Gen. 17:

5-8] God then announced that Sarai, Abram's wife, renamed to be *Sarah*, was to bear Abraham a son named Isaac. It was through Abraham's faith, guidance and obedience to God's testing of him that he was willing to obey God's request of Abraham to sacrifice Isaac. It was in the act of that sacrifice that God called, "Abraham, Abraham!" And Abraham said, "Here am I." God said, "Do not lay your hand on the lad or do anything to him; for now I know that you fear God, seeing you have not withheld your son, your only son, from Me." [Gen. 22: 11-12] In Verse 13, Abraham saw a ram caught by the horns in a thicket. That ram's sacrifice was God's reinstatement of His reprieve, or covering over sin that was to continue as the constant reminder of mankind's dependence on God's continuing grace. God protects and rescues life, but not always as in the case of God's only Son, Jesus. Jesus' mission was to establish a new covenant, which was to be sealed in blood. To rescue Jesus, the testing of our faith would make His coming into this world meaningless insofar as for man's sin. The losing of a loved one is for testing and trusting, like Abraham's test.

THE EXODUS

The next major step in God's leading a nation to greatness in servant hood is in the exodus of the Hebrew people from Egypt, led by Moses. In bringing Moses to leadership of a nation of people, God brought deliverance from destruction and death, to a nation of people by the Holy Spirit. God's Spirit worked in Moses' upbringing, his education, his separation and experience in the desert, his reintroduction to his people, and the experience of a burning bush and call by God to lead His (God's) chosen people.

It was God's Spirit that worked the miracles that released the Hebrew nation from Egypt. It was God's Spirit that protected them by day in a "pillar of cloud" and by night in a "pillar of fire." [Exodus 14: 19]

The escape was climaxed at the parting of the sea. [Exodus 14: 24] The Spirit of God hovered over His people providing food in the form of ". . . a fine, flake-like thing, fine as hoarfrost on the ground. When the people of Israel saw it, they said to one another, 'What is it?' for they did not know what it was. And Moses said to them, 'It is bread which the Lord has given you to eat.'" [Exodus 16: 146-151] What God had given them was the sustenance of life also which holds true when Jesus blessed the bread; it is the sustenance of the new life in Jesus' service.

What it Means to be Born from Above

The Hebrew nation wandered in the wilderness,
protected and guided by the Holy Spirit through Moses

GOD'S REBELLIOUS PEOPLE

That leadership of the God's Spirit continued with the Hebrew nation, but because the spirit of the Hebrews was still wandering, their appetites ruled, because of that they remained disobedient, resulting in forty years' in the wilderness. It is also in the wilderness experience that Moses was summoned to the top of Mt. Sinai. [Exodus 19: 20] It was at Mt. Sinai that God spoke the words, "I am the Lord your God, who brought you out of the land of Egypt, out of the hours of bondage."

RULES OF LIFE

God continued by telling Moses the ten rules the Hebrew nation was to govern their lives by and the way of life in faithfulness to God. "You shall have no other gods before Me. [Exodus 20:3] This commandment stresses unity. "You shall not make for yourself graven images. . ." [Exodus 20:4] This commandment stresses the spirituality of God. "You shall not take the name of your Lord God in vain. . ." [Exodus 20:7] This third commandment forbids the degrading and cheap use of the divine. "Remember the Sabbath Day, to keep it holy. [Exodus 20:8] This commandment stresses the need to remember and celebrate God's intervention, protection, sustaining and ongoing guiding power of the Holy Spirit of God.

"Honor your father and mother." [Exodus 20:12] This commandment points to the importance of family as a solid framework for support, team effort, and unified faith and worship of God the Father of all creation. "You shall not kill." [Exodus 20:13] This commandment stresses that God and God alone has the right to give and take life. "You shall not commit adultery." [Exodus 20:14] This commandment focuses on the bonding of two earthly spirits with one

Heavenly Spirit resulting in one union in trust, loyalty and love.

"You shall not steal." [Exodus 20:15] This commandment underscores the right to have and keep what you earn in honest labor; no one has the right to it, lest you freely give it away. The tithe is the freely given gift in response to having received. "You shall not bear false witness against your neighbor" [Exodus 20:16]. This commandment lays out the importance of "truth-telling." Falsehoods always are ferreted out and the truth prevails. "You shall not covet your neighbor's house. . ." [Exodus 20:17] This commandment tries to draw man away from things that only draw him away from God. If one is to covet, covet righteousness [Matt. 5:6]. This draws man to God.

These do's and don'ts were to guide God's people in how to live, how to build a solid bond in trust and love with their fellow sojourners and with God -- the God who relentlessly pursues His creation with love and forgiveness. The one thing the Hebrews lacked in order to put all this together as God's chosen people was God's Spirit on an individual level, this lack of power to overcome the drive to satisfy the desires of the flesh. The separation of man's spirit and God's Spirit made it difficult for the Hebrews to connect with God.

God seemed to be up there somewhere, the One on top of a Holy Mountain called Mt. Sinai.

A HOUSE FOR GOD

After all, the Hebrews were God's chosen people: "For you are a people holy to the Lord your God; the Lord your God has chosen you to be a people for His own possession . . ." [Exodus 19:25 and Deuteronomy 7:6]

That prompted God to say, "Let them make me a sanctuary, that I may dwell in their midst." [Exodus 25:8] God then laid out the plans for what is to be called, "The Tabernacle in the Wilderness." "They shall make an ark of acacia wood." [Deut. 10] He then gave instructions on its size and ornateness. Later, we learn that the ark was to house the Ten Commandments. [Exodus 10: 5]

This was God's attempt to move from "up there" to "down here" -- God's attempt to make His chosen people feel that God was among them, but still separate.

John, in all the affluence he enjoyed, felt down deep that something was lacking. He tried to fill his life with things, like a new watch, but the emptiness continued. John's father was often away earning the money that made life easy. When his father was home, he showed little attention to John. This emptiness grew to the point of despair – suicide.

One night, when there was nothing left for John, with a gun in his hand, he got a call from his father. At the time he was in another city. Separated by distance, but close via phone, the father called to say, "I was thinking about you and how much you make a difference in my life. I love you very much." John put the gun down, and from that point on, his life was renewed – because of love.

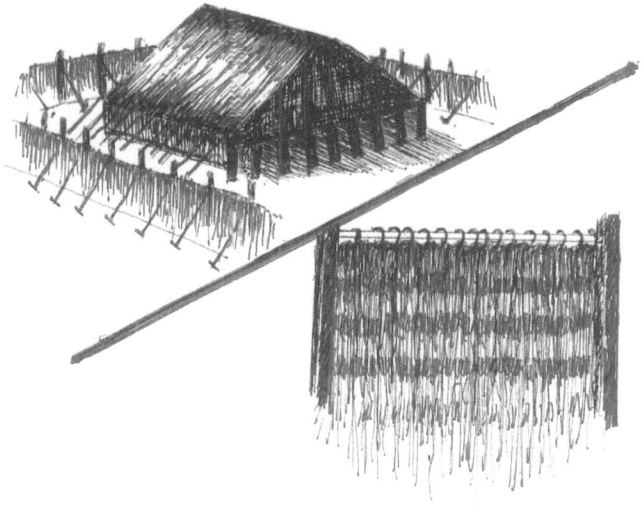

    a. The tabernacle in the wilderness.
b. Veil that separated the Holy of Holies, the place where God resided when He was separated from His people.

Chapter 26 of Exodus begins the instructions for the building of the Tabernacle in the Wilderness. The Tabernacle in the Wilderness consisted of three major spaces: the outer court, now called the foyer, a large area where the people gathered; the sanctuary now called the nave where only the priests were to enter; and the Holy of Holies where God resided along with the Ten Commandments housed in the Ark (which also represented the Mercy Seat). God expressed what was to happen in the Holy of Holies: "Aaron shall make atonement upon its [the Ark's] horns once a year; with blood of the sin offering of atonement." [Exodus 30:10] The Holy of Holies was separated from the priest and the people by a heavy veil. "And you shall make a veil of blue and purple and scarlet stuff and fine twined linen . . . ." [Exodus 26:31] The only one who could enter the Holy of Holies was the High Priest, and then only once a year.

The priests carried out their rituals on a daily basis only in the sanctuary, i.e. burning incense, trimming the lamps on a seven-branched lamp stand, and making animal sacrifices for the sins of the people.

THE DAY OF ATONEMENT

On the Day of Atonement, the one day the High Priest was allowed in the Holy of Holies which housed the Ark of the Covenant that contained the Ten Commandments constituting the Mercy Seat, a special ritual was performed. "And he [the High Priest] shall make atonement for the sanctuary and for the altar and he shall make atonement for the priests and for all the people of the assembly." [Leviticus 16:33]

That act of atonement covered all the bases. It was one grand day in which all things and all people were cleansed, so that the relationship between God and Israel should continue unbroken – all this even though mankind continued rejecting God's efforts for reconciliation. The Hebrews could not connect with God personally. God was in their midst, but separated by a veil. God in a sense was there.

The proceedings on the Day of Atonement began with everyone fasting – the whole nation, even the children. The Day of Atonement comes ten days after the opening of the Jewish New Year, called "Yom Kippur." Very early in the morning the High Priest cleansed himself by washing. He then donned gorgeous robes of his office as described in Exodus [28]. Those robes were worn only on that one day.

There were white linen breeches and a long white undergarment reaching to his feet, woven in one piece. There was "the Robe of the Ephod." The Ephod is thought to be the oldest article of apparel connected with worship. No one really knows what it was. But the robe under it was dark blue and was long with a fringe of blue, purple and scarlet tassels made in the form of pomegranates, interspersed with an equal number of little golden bells. The Ephod was put on over the blue robe. It was thought to be a linen tunic. On its shoulders were two onyx stones. The names of six of tribes were on one shoulder and the other six tribes were on the other. On the linen tunic, there was a "breast plate," a "span square." On it were twelve precious stones each representing one of the twelve tribes, with their names engraved on it. The High Priest thereby carried the people to God on his shoulders and on his heart. On his head the High Priest put the tall "Miter," of fine linen, and on the Miter was a gold plate bordered by a band of blue ribbon, and on the plate were the words, "Holiness unto the Lord."

Continuing on in Chapter 29, once he dressed in the special garb, he began his duties. First he performed what he did every day as described above. When his daily duties were completed, he began the special ritual for the Day of

Atonement. It should be noted here that the priest was one who represented God to the people and the people to God. He did not make atonement, but was the mediator through which God gives atonement. Here again God is, as with Adam and Eve, covering over (a reprieve) of man's sin.

Still dressed in his magnificent robes, he sacrificed a bullock, seven lambs and one ram as described in Numbers 29:7. Then he removed his robes, cleansed himself again in water, and redressed himself in the simple purity of white linen. At that point, a bullock was brought to him that had been bought with his own resources. He placed his hands on its head, and standing there in full sight of the people, he confessed his own sin and the sins of his house. His prayer was, "O, Lord God, I have committed iniquity; I have transgressed; I have sinned, I and my house. O Lord, I entreat you, cover over [atone for, reprieve] the iniquities, the transgressions and the sins which I have committed, transgressed, and sinned before you. I and my house even as it is written in the Law of Moses, Your servant, 'for on that day he will cover [atone] for you to make you clean from all your transgressions before the Lord, you shall be cleansed.'"

The priest left the bullock and went to two goats that were brought to him. Two lots were drawn and one was placed on the head of one goat and one on the other. One lot read *Jehovah* and the other read *Azazel*, which means "The Scapegoat." The Priest then turned to the bullock and killed it by cutting its throat. The blood was caught in a basin. Then the priest took burning coals from the altar and dropped them into a censer. He took the burning incense and the basin of blood and walked into the Holy of Holies to burn incense in the presence of God. He put down the incense and the basin quickly because he must not tarry long – lest he die. He came out and showed the assembly he was OK and returned into the Holy of Holies to sprinkle the blood from the basin seven times over the altar. Next he brought out the remaining blood in the basin, killed the goat marked, *Jehovah*. The blood from that goat, which is the seat of life, was mingled with the blood of the bullock in the basin. Following that, he returned to the Holy of Holies and sprinkled the altar again. Next, he came out and sprinkled the altar in the sanctuary, cleansing it – thus, cleansing both the altar and the Holy of Holies. The scapegoat was brought forward. The High Priest laid his hand on it and confessed his own sin and the sin of the people, and the goat was then driven into the desert, "into a land not inhabited," laden with the sins of the people. There it was killed.

Nothing has changed. We still look for someone or something or some situation to blame for whatever it is that we want to excuse. Scapegoating abounds -- "It's their fault I did this." When situations get tough we hear, "We are in this fix because of those greedy people out there!" We look for some others rather than ourselves to determine the root of our problems – our scapegoat.

Finally, the High Priest read scripture, performed a few more rituals to finish the ceremony. Thus ended the ritual of the Day of Atonement, the day designed to cleanse all things and all people of sin. Every year the ritual had to be performed, again and again and again. The sacrifice was that of bulls and goats and their blood. The whole thing failed because such things cannot atone for sin on the inside. It requires more than external rituals, but a transformation of the whole person, inside and out. Also, there was no guarantee that the bullock or the goats or the blood were not defiled, which made the whole ritual null and void. Atonement (at-one-ment through sacrifice) required a guaranteed pure and blameless sacrifice – and that comes in the form of Jesus, the only Son of God, incarnate – both internally and externally and once and for all. The total redemption comes later, but until that event took place, the Hebrew people had to trust the High Priest and the rituals to be authentic means of atonement. God was still using the animal sacrifice to cover over sin -- a reprieve.

The Tabernacle, the Ark, and the Ten Commandments gave assurance to the Hebrew people that the Lord God of Creation and His Holy Spirit was among them and leading them. When the Hebrew nation moved with the Ark containing the Ten Commandments leading the way, the Hebrews were protected by the Holy Spirit and victorious in their quest for the Promised Land [Joshua 6: 1-21]. Here we are told that the walls of Jericho were destroyed.

GOD'S PROTECTION AND DELIVERANCE

That empowerment of the Hebrew armies was by God's Spirit, God's ongoing protection and deliverance of His Chosen People, enabling them to defeat their enemies. That continued until the Hebrew army faced a Philistine giant [I Samuel 17: 3-11], "And there came out from the camp of the Philistines a champion named Goliath . . . ." Verses 10 and 11 read, "I defy the ranks of Israel this day; give me a man, that we may fight together." When Saul and all Israel heard these words of the Philistine, they were dismayed and greatly afraid. Why was the powerful army of Israel afraid? Here was an army that has defeated every enemy up to that time. What may be said is that Israel became proud, full or themselves and forgot that God's Holy Spirit was their protector. It was at that point that God's Spirit left the army and entered a lad named David, son of Jesse. As mentioned earlier, David was called to battle the Philistine giant, saying, "The Lord, who delivered me from the paw of the lion and from the paw of the bear, will deliver me from the hand of this Philistine." [I Samuel 17:37] David recognized the indwelling of the power of the Holy Spirit and had the knowledge he would be protected in order to defeat the Philistine. David was a good shot with a sling, but it was the Holy Spirit that made sure the stone hit the right spot.

JESUS – THE EMBODIMENT OF GOD

It was stated earlier that God created humankind's spirit in the beginning and later formed a structure we call a body in order to care for the rest of His creation. That incarnation of man's spirit is the beginning of a lineage leading to God's ultimate incarnation, Jesus. Jesus was conceived by the Holy Spirit to be incarnate in human form. [Matthew 1:18-20]. As in Genesis where Adam and Eve's spirits walked with God's Spirit, Jesus was also in the company of God's Spirit, as though they are one. "Hear, O Israel: the Lord our God is One." [Rev. 6:4]

On the other hand, unlike Adam and Eve, who disobeyed God, Jesus remained in a deep relationship with God. In spite of their disobedience, God protected them, as God protected Jesus from Herod's desire to destroy any and all competition. Also, unlike Adam and Eve who did not fully understand the relationship they had with God, and did not understand the lasting consequence of their exercising free will in the favor of their own appetites, Jesus was fully aware of the relationship He had with His Father in Heaven. Even at the early age of 12 we read in Luke 2:49, "And he said to them, 'How is it that you [Mary and Joseph] sought me? Did you not know that I must be in my Father's house?'" Jesus had entered fully into our humanity [Hebrews 2:14ff] and succeeded in being obedient even unto death on a cross. [Philippians 2:8] Adam and Eve, and all those who followed up to the time of Jesus, were not able to be fully obedient.

From the age of 12 to age 30, there is no record of Jesus' upbringing or His relationship with God. Many stories have been told concerning this period, but for this author, those years were spent experiencing the human condition – the pain, the joy, the frustration of having limited resources, all for the knowledge needed to minister to His Father's Creation, and to us [cf. Heb. 5:8-9]. Having that education and having compassion at the age when it was possible to enter the priesthood or to become a Rabbi, Jesus sought out His cousin, John the Baptist in the wilderness. John had been preaching repentance of sin and baptism to the Hebrew people. [Matthew 3:1-3] John declared, ". . . Prepare the way of the Lord, make His path straight." [Matthew 3:3] He announced, "I baptize you with water for repentance [an external cleansing], but He who is coming after me is mightier than I, whose sandals I am not worthy to carry. He will baptize you with the Holy Spirit . . . ." [Matthew 3:11]

This was the "internal cleansing" resulting in the complete external and internal redemption.

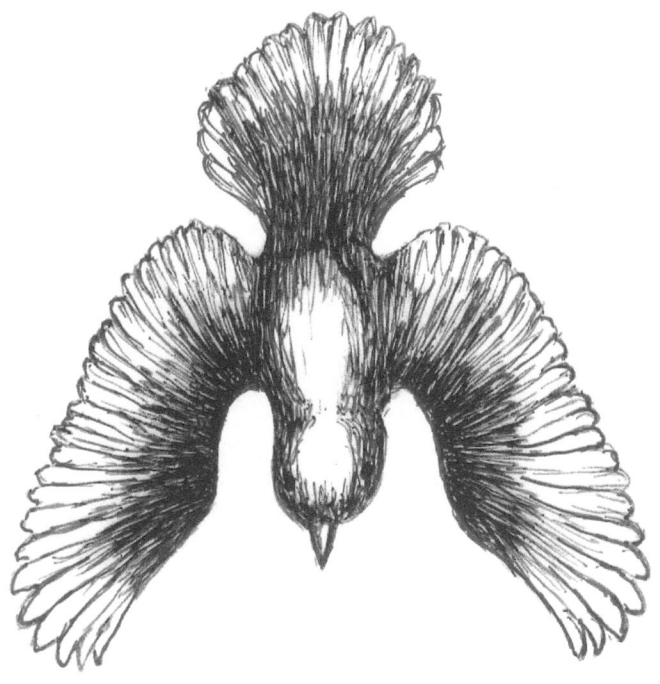

The descending dove symbolizing God's Holy Spirit
entering Jesus at His baptism.

JESUS ENDOWED WITH THE SPIRIT

Jesus came to John and said, "Let it be so now, for thus it is fitting for us to fulfill all righteousness." John baptized Him and, "The Spirit of God descending like a dove, alighting on Him . . . ." [Matthew 3:16] Whereas, by contrast, God, when confronting Adam and Eve with their disobedience that resulted in a spiritual rejection, Jesus was praised for his obedience: "Lo, a voice from heaven came saying, 'This is my beloved Son, with whom I am well pleased . . . .'" [Matthew 3:16]

Where Adam and Eve failed by turning away from God, Jesus embraced God and followed faithfully, as the temptation account shows. Jesus, armed with the Holy Spirit and the acceptance of His Father, entered His test and succeeded. "Then Jesus was led up by the Spirit into the wilderness to be tempted by the devil." [Matthew 4:1].

The temptation was not to destroy Jesus' obedience, but to show the power of the Holy Spirit overcoming the desire to turn away from God to pleasure, our own egos and desires. Jesus held fast to the guidance and power of the Holy Spirit and proclaimed, "You shall worship the Lord your God and Him only shall you serve." [Matthew 4:10] Jesus did what

Adam and Eve did not do and later could not do, that was to make things right. That leads to the thought that Jesus is a "Second Adam." God started His disclosure to mankind with Adam and Eve and disappointed to the point of wishing He (God) had not started the project [Genesis 6:6]. Finding favor with Noah, God tried to wipe the slate clean with a flood, then started over hoping for a better outcome by issuing a covenant not to destroy the Earth again. Later, God found favor in Abraham and established another new covenant with His people. God had kept His end of each of His covenants, but humanity had not.

A NEW COVENANT

Now, for the third time, God began the process of establishing a final new covenant, *"KAINOS,"* through Jesus. "And He took the cup, and when He had given thanks, He gave it to them saying, 'Drink of it, all of you; for this is my blood of the covenant (*KAINOS*), which is poured out for many for the forgiveness of sins.'" [Matthew 26:27, 28]

The New Covenant was based on the power of the life-giving Holy Spirit that created humankind in the beginning and now presents the risen Christ to us and opens our hearts and lives to receive Him. God lifted the reprieve that covered over sin from the beginning and now in Jesus' sacrifice, replaced that reprieve with a "total pardon" for repented sin when man enters the new covenant through Jesus the Christ. Repented sin can be achieved because this covenant provides both the external and internal cleansing. Water baptism cleanses the outside; the Holy Spirit cleanses the inside. The dying to an old life, rising to a new life dedicated to service in thanksgiving for the life-giving power of God. In this new relationship with God our Father as His children we are no longer criminals in default. The new covenant not only changes people, but gives them the strength and the knowledge to accomplish God's will. They have the power to meet and control the temptations to turn away from God and indulge in ego-centered disobedience, just as Jesus remained obedient using the power of the Holy Spirit.

This gives us a "leg up" on Adam and Eve. We now know if we own up to our mistakes, because of the new covenant, in and through Jesus' life and death, we are forgiven. Unlike Adam and Eve, we fully understand the consequences of our disobedience, thus making us doubly accountable.

THE GIFT OF THE SPIRIT

It is the same Holy Spirit that empowered Jesus to resist temptation, and by God's grace, it is ours as well. The Holy Spirit gave Jesus insight into men and women's hearts, to have healing power, and to have the authority to forgive sin, and to represent the living presence of God in our midst.

Max Lucado, in his book, *Just Like Jesus* makes reference to the job of a translator. A translator allows the message of the speaker to flow through him or her. When the speaker is loud, the translator is loud, when he or she is soft, the translator is soft; when the speaker gestures, the translator gestures.

A parallel is made, "When Jesus walked the earth, Jesus was God's translator -- translating God all the time. When God got louder, Jesus got louder. When God gestured, Jesus gestured. He was so in sync with the Father that He could declare, "I am in the Father and the Father in me . . . " [John 14:11]. The Holy Spirit, the power of God, ties God the Father and God the Son so tightly together that Jesus and God become one. And through Jesus' resurrection we too are taken into this union [John 17:1-26].

What it Means to be Born from Above

Jesus makes the final blood sacrifice for sin, establishing the new covenant that all who repent their sin, profess their belief in Jesus as the Christ, the only Son of God, and are baptized, symbolizing the commitment to walk in Christ-like life.

It was the same Holy Spirit that gave Jesus the strength to say in the Garden just before His arrest, "My Father, if it be possible, let this cup pass from me; nevertheless, not as I will [ego], but as Thou wilt." [Matthew 26:39] The death of Jesus the Christ was God's last sacrifice for sin. Where we are not able to accomplish total atonement, God does it for us in and through Jesus the Christ [see II Cor. 5:19]. God made the first sacrifice to cover over sins; God now makes the last sacrifice to pardon us of our sins and makes this real and effective in us through the Holy Spirit becoming present and active in our hearts and lives.

The veil is rent in the temple letting God out and the people in.

The veil that separated God and the people in the temple was rent from top to bottom, "And behold, the curtain of the temple was torn in two, from top to bottom . . . ." [Matthew 27:51] That event ended the separation of God and his people. The ripping of the veil allowed God out into our midst, and human beings into God's presence, making it real for us to be connected to God by the Holy Spirit and allowing us to emulate Jesus as God's translator.

The ascending Christ – by rising from the watery grave
as Jesus the Christ was raised from the tomb – to life a new and
changed life in the service of God, walking in Christ.

EMPOWERMENT BY THE SPIRIT

In the book of Acts of the Apostles of the New Testament, we read of the Holy Spirit, ". . . until the day when He [Jesus] was taken up, after He (Jesus) had given commandment through the Holy Spirit to the apostles whom He had chosen, He was taken up to Heaven." [Acts 1:2] Jesus asked the disciples just before His ascension to remain in Jerusalem for ". . . you shall receive power when the Holy Spirit has come upon you; and you shall be my witnesses in Jerusalem and all of Judea and Samaria and to the end of the Earth."

[Acts 1:6-8] The disciples then learned the truth of Jesus' promise . . . "When the day of Pentecost had come, they were all together in one place. And suddenly a sound came from heaven like the rush of a mighty wind, and it filled all the house where they were sitting. And there appeared to them tongues as of fire, distributed and resting on each one of them. And they were filled with the Holy Spirit and began to speak in other tongues as the Spirit gave them utterance." [Acts 2: 1-4]

The disciples, individually and as a community (the church), became new creatures, born anew, or born from above, if you will, to do and be the ongoing transformation of the world from what it was and is to what God wants it to be in the future, to be true and faithful translators of the love of God. It is you and all followers of Jesus the Christ our Savior, who are willing to realize our death to sin and resurrection to a new life through water baptism, the cleansing, that we receive the baptism of the Holy Spirit that empowers us to fulfill our mission of proclaiming the saving acts of our Creator God and Father.

Because of God's grace, love and compassion, the Holy Spirit that once walked with Adam and Eve, later to be withdrawn, is now reunited with us on a personal level as it was in the very beginning. Through Jesus and the Holy Spirit, God recreates us spiritually as a whole, both physically and spiritually [Eph. 4:17 ff] giving us new birth, a new focus on life, a new lifestyle, a new objective and purpose. That new purpose is to serve God.

INSTANTANEOUS OR GRADUAL REBIRTH?

The new birth, or being born from above, may occur as a life changing event, taking place quickly or more gradually over time as the formation of a new lifestyle or way of life. The quick change for some has a point to which one can refer and say, "That's when I was born from above." For others the new birth may be quick but not realized fully for a longer period of time, with no specific point of time. What is important is that the lifestyle, thought patterns and attitudes change from self-service to serving God the Father through Jesus the Christ. The indwelling of the Holy Spirit allows us to feel and act as Martin Luther did, before the "Diet of Worms," when he said, "Here I stand. I can do no other."

WALKING WITH THE SPIRIT

So how do we know if we are truly born from above, that the Holy Spirit is in fact a part of our lives? Let's review the actions of those who walked with God or were led by the Holy Spirit.

Adam and Eve walked with God, led by the Spirit which was united with them until their disobedience and the withdrawal of the guiding Spirit as we read in Genesis 2. In Genesis 6:5 we read of God's displeasure at what human beings had done, but found one who remained in God's favor (Genesis 6:8).

". . . . but Noah found favor in the eyes of God." Noah was walking with God. Then, in Genesis 17:1, Abram, later to be named Abraham, walked with God's Spirit, "I am God Almighty; walk before me, and be blameless." Abraham went so far in walking in the Spirit that he was willing to sacrifice his own son, Isaac. (Genesis 22:1).

Moses was another man who responded and walked with the Spirit of God. Exodus 3:12 reads, "He [God] said, "But I will be with you and this shall be the sign for you that I have sent you . . . ." The Spirit of God, when walking with His creation, gives His creation what it needs to accomplish His ultimate goal. God sends Moses out, saying, "Now therefore go, and I will be with your mouth and teach you what you shall speak." (Exodus 4:12).

God's Spirit walked with the many prophets of the Old Testament in the ongoing edification of His will for His creation. Some succeeded to a degree while others failed. Then came God's ace in the hand, His Son Jesus. Jesus walked faithfully with the Spirit, climaxing in the statement made by God the Father of us all, "This is my beloved Son with whom I am well pleased." (Matthew 3:17) So how do we know if we are truly born from above, that the Holy Spirit is in fact a part of our lives? How do we know that we are also, as all those before us, walking with the Holy Spirit?

Look at the overall picture of events in one's life. Many of these events while walking with the Spirit of God are the ultimate goal of God's ongoing revelation. They have always been stepping stones leading to God's ultimate goal that is having all of His creation walking with the Holy Spirit.

Lee's publishing of sacramental certificates had come to a place that a decision had to be made whether to continue or stop. Due to desktop publishing, churches have opted to create and publish their own materials. Enter the Holy Spirit. Lee grew up in South Florida where coral rock was indigenous to his landscape. When red brick, Kentucky field stone, and Vermont Granite began to adorn houses, he felt those imports did not fit. After several years, Lee recreated simulated coral rock out of cement. It looked and felt just like the real thing. Lee decided to mold this into ornamental block, which in turn was used to make eight foot crosses with colored resin is the spaces of the blocks that captured the light causing the cross to glow.

It was in the forming and the filling the block one day that after making sure there was no rain in the forecast that the Holy Spirit stepped in. Lee had been told that water and resin do not mix. Resin was used to fill pockets formed into the block. This allowed the light to shine through the block. Lee checked since they were outside, that there was no rain in the area. Lee poured the resin into 12 blocks. He no sooner had poured the last block when a small cloud appeared and rain began. It had not rained in several weeks and did not rain again for two weeks after this very short shower. Lee quickly threw a tarp over the block in an attempt to save the resin from the rain. Several hours later after the resin was expected to have hardened, Lee removed the tarp only to find the covering had leaked water into every block leaving puddles of water in the resin. "Oh, No! Ruined!" was the response to the situation—four weeks of work down the drain. Lee lifted the block and poured the water out to discover the water had formed round circles of various sizes in the resin. Also, when lifting the block to allow the light to shine through the circles, the effect of the resin was better than expected. Immediately, Lee said, "I had a good idea, but God had a better idea." Now Lee, when making the block for a cross, pours water into the resin to force circles. Thank you, Lord.

Looking at the overall picture of one's life, one must pray for forgiveness of sin and for cleansing. "To live from a new knowing," is a principle set forth by Dr. Wayne Dyer in his lecture on "Being in Balance." He continues to say that each of us who has been born from above needs to say, "I know that now I have an invisible connection to God and that now defines me, and I now have a divine guidance available to me."

This knowing, he continues, brings those who are born-from-above into balance, "a balance that allows them to die while they are still alive, . . . but having the option of choosing to live in true and enlightened balance of God's realignment now in this physical state." .

This knowing of the comprehensive love of God for each and every human being He has made available to each one. The realignment of Spirit fosters a feeling of gratitude and a sense that it is an honor to be a part of this creation. That is what Dr. Dyer calls "being in Spirit." Such being-in-Spirit allows us to gain the insight of knowing the workings and guidance of the Holy Spirit as it is happening. We acknowledge the Holy Spirit in action instantly. We become change agents. As the old saying goes, "When you change the way you see and treat people, people change."

This change is sometimes quick and sometimes takes a while. It is easy to look back to see His guiding force. The trick is to see it when it happens. To be Christ-like, that is to be aware and constantly in the presence of God, we need to make a conscious effort to recognize Him in all things at all times. Even in adverse times, give thanks, because there is a positive lesson to learn that leads to better understanding of God's will.

Has there been a radical change or a gradual change in one's objectives, desires and actions from self-centeredness to seeking and serving God through love, compassion and forgiveness? To answer that listen to Paul's words, "For the desires of the flesh are against the spirit, and the desires of the

Spirit are against the flesh... now the works of the flesh are plain: immorality, impurity, licentiousness, idolatry, sorcery, enmity, strife, jealousy, anger, selfishness, dissention, party spirit, envy, drunkenness, carousing and the like." [Galatians 5: 17-24] Paul further warns, "... those who do such things shall not inherit the Kingdom of God." This is true if the Spirit is not present and man turns away from God. But when the Spirit is requested to enter the heart and is present and active, a transformation of the flesh takes place, either quickly or gradually and the body and spirit work together so that "The fruit of the Spirit [coupled with humankind] is love, joy, peace, patience, kindness, goodness, faithfulness, gentleness, self-control ... ," Paul continues. Here is the yardstick that measures where one stands in regard to whether the Holy Spirit is present in one's life. Having said all this, in the last analysis, only God really knows who is truly born from above; even the most saintly must pray for forgiveness of sin and for cleansing.

Lee's ministry had been to small congregations of less than 80 active members, and that made it hard to make a wage large enough to support a growing family. Lee's ministry became a "tent ministry," much like Paul of Tarsus. This was made possible by God's guiding Spirit, when He guided Lee into partnership with a printer. Why a printing company? It opened the door for Lee to create tools for the Christian ministry that otherwise was not possible. Lee realized immediately that what seemed a side-track at first was God's way of equipping His servant with the tools to accomplish the will of God for building the Kingdom. Lee began a 30 year publishing company, providing worship aids for the Christian ministry.

In Galatians 6:7 Paul writes, "Do not be deceived; God is not mocked, for whatever a man sows, that he will also reap. For he who sows to his own flesh will from the flesh reap corruption, but he who sows to the Spirit will from the Spirit reap eternal life." [Galatians 6:7]

So why did Jesus say to Nicodemus that he had to be born from above? This is why -- being "born from above" means acknowledging the Holy Spirit as the transforming power of God made available through the life, death and resurrection of Jesus the Christ, our Savior, who made our lives as our guiding force, transforming our lives, either overnight or over a long period of time, to be the example of the fruit of the Spirit. Let it be so for you!

BEING IN CHRIST

Up to this point, the term "Holy Spirit" has been used as it belongs to God, and "spirit" is used as it belongs to humankind. Dr. Wayne Dyer uses the term "In Spirit". Being "in spirit" refers to man's spirit as guided by what Dr. Dyer terms, our "Source," or God the Father. Now let us draw our attention to Paul's letter to the Romans, Chapter 6, where Paul writes of walking with Christ in "newness of life." Baptism in its truest form is shedding the life that leads away from God and taking on a life that leads to God. One universally accepted truth is that in order to overcome any of life's difficulties, one needs a support system. It might be an institution, a group, family members, or a community of faith. The ultimate support is from God. That support is available only through Jesus the Christ.

Being in Christ is when one is united with Christ. In verse 5 of Chapter 6 of Romans, Paul writes, ". . . for if we have been united with Him in a death like His, we shall certainly be united with Him in a resurrection like His." In baptism we have been united with Christ. In the Gospel of John 15:1-8, Jesus speaks of his being the vine and we who are baptized are the branches. When Paul writes that we have been united with Christ, it means that we "have been grafted in" so that we can grow together.

Citrus growers know that the "graft" does not bear fruit immediately; it grows to maturity gradually and is identified with the host plant. In our case, when we are grafted into Christ in Baptism, we begin a gradual period of time that never ceases to grow. As long as water and fertilizer are supplied to the grafted citrus tree, it produces delicious fruit. When it is not maintained with those requirements, it dies. It is so with us; if we cease to feed on the word of God and fail to follow in the footsteps of Christ, we wither and die spiritually. If God is a spirit, we are spirits in a physical body, and our spirits are capable from the beginning of walking with God's spirit. But, because God's spirit is so difficult for our human minds to comprehend, He mercifully provided a means of fellowship with Him through His Son, Jesus the Christ.

For 30 years, Jesus experienced the life of a human being. He spent three more years teaching the attributes of compassion, love and care for others. He paved the way for us to travel a safe and blessed journey through life "grafted" to Him. His ultimate act was to open the door for us to enter into the Holy of Holies sinless. He went to the cross to pay the price we could not do for ourselves. Now through His love and sacrifice we can be born from above through baptism into newness of life. Guided by the Holy Spirit we fulfill God's intention for the creation of humankind.

CONCLUSION

An artist recognizes another's work because each and every time an artist has a style that is all his or her own. That is to say, an artist's personality is in his or her work. One can say even further that you cannot separate the artist from his or her works.

In the beginning, God created all things, and if one cannot separate the artist from his or her works, and then one cannot separate God from His creation. God's stamp is all over His creation, and "it was all good." This being true, it must also be true that the way we treat His creation is how we treat God.

When God's Holy Spirit walked with Adam's and Eve's spirits, all was in harmony. When Adam and Eve disobeyed by exercising their free will to accept or reject God's rules, they ushered in disharmony. That did not cause God to withdraw His love of His creation. It only caused Him to take another method to teach and express His love. He had to force the humans to examine themselves and how they relate to God our Father and how we treat Him. However, because humans don't fully understand life, love, grace, forgiveness and trust, they were not able to reconcile themselves to God. What did remain with us was the intense desire to seek out a god, not necessarily the One God, but that mysterious force greater than ourselves. Therefore, trees, rocks, heavenly bodies were worshiped as natural or mythical figures in temporary terms. While in the wilderness, the Hebrews, God's Chosen People, after all His protection and provisions lost their belief in the guidance of God. They turned back to a "Golden Calf" as their god. In all disloyalty, the love of God for His creation and His chosen people remained in the dark recesses of the hearts of mankind. It is this author's opinion that God is inside each of us wanting to come forth, much like the example of the veil in the Tabernacle in the Wilderness that separated God from the people. Jesus the Christ's sacrifice to pay our sinful debt opens the door for baptized believers' spirits to be reunited with the Holy Spirit.

To illustrate, a national bank sends a letter stating that you can have a credit line of $5,000. All you have to do is fill out the enclosed form and send it in. You do as instructed. A few weeks later you receive another letter which contains a plastic card with your name and a 16 digit number on it. The letter states you now have a $5,000 credit line. But, before you can exercise the $5,000 worth of purchasing power, you have to do is call a certain phone number that is printed on a sticker on the front of the card. The phone call activates the card's ability to draw on your line of credit. The power to buy merchandise is yours, available to you for the period of time stated on the card. But, before you can draw on it, you have to validate the card.

The saving power of God's Holy Spirit is like the bank card. We are notified by teachers and prophets that it is available to us. All we have to do to activate that love, grace and power is to accept Jesus the Christ, be baptized showing our total commitment, to die to an old life (cleansing) and rise to a new life filled and governed by the Holy Spirit.

Every time we meet around the Communion Table we affirm the life and death of Jesus. By taking the bread, we affirm the physical manifestation of God in Jesus. Jesus shed the physical, just as we will, so as to free us from that bondage. The physical is bound to one place and time and is also the source of sin when it is unchecked and leaderless. By participating in the breaking of bread, we recognize Jesus' sacrifice "the once-and-for-all death" releasing us from the debt of sin. We symbolically join Him by remembering Him. The tearing of the bread symbolizes the tearing of the veil in the temple, letting God out and humankind in to the Holy of Holies. It is the sacrifice that Jesus made that allows us into the presence of God, strengthened by the Holy Spirit.

When we partake of the "cup" containing fluids that symbolize the blood of Jesus, we affirm the life-giving qualities of the Holy Spirit.

Covenants are often written documents spelling out undying commitments. The ultimate covenant is giving one's life in blood. This covenant is the kind that God makes with us through Jesus. "Drink of it, all of you; for this is my blood of the covenant, which is poured out for many for the forgiveness of sin." (Matthew 26; 27-28). This act of communion celebrates the death to sin and the rising to a new life. We keep in good standing with the power of the Holy Spirit, just as we did when we professed our faith before the world and was grafted in to the body of Christ.

If one fails to follow the rules of one's credit card by not making payments the card is withdrawn and the balance continues to accumulate interest, making the debt greater. The same holds true with one's new life in Christ as a new creation. We can renew and activate our credit card by paying back payments and interest. It is so with our new life. We can renew our relationship on a daily basis by prayer, reading Scripture and on a weekly basis by communal worship of God celebrating the greatest gift of the forgiveness of sin through the sacrifice of Jesus the Christ reenacted in Holy Communion.

The so-called "Holy Grail," the cup from which Jesus drank at the Last Supper, which many believe still exists somewhere, will never be found. For hundreds of years the faithful have searched for it without success – because it is hidden in plain sight. It is you and me!

We are to take in the bread, symbolizing the food that strengthens our bodies for service, and the wine, symbolizing the blood of Jesus that strengthens our spiritual bodies. He initiated this communion with Him at the Last Supper in order to cleanse us both physically and spiritually to continue the ongoing work where He left off. We are to pour ourselves out like Jesus did so that others may eat and drink of the saving power of a loving God through the Holy Spirit.

By acceptance of Jesus as the Son of our Living God, through baptism in the name of the Father, the Son and the

Holy Spirit, we have said to this world that we have invited that Holy Spirit to empower us. In addition, we have said we have turned our will over to the will of God. He is now the controller of our lives. Our new birth is now into God's family, governed by His rules and not our own. We are now vessels of saving power to be poured out so that all who seek a new life may be fed and receive the blessings we have been given.

We celebrate our birth into this world each year, the birth that was not of our choosing. However, we no not celebrate each year the rite of birth that was our decision, that of our belief in Jesus the Christ as our Savior. At the time of baptism we enter a new life and die to the old. When we are born "from above" in good standing, we will be living eternally in the presence of God. Otherwise, we will spend eternity separated from God. Our decision to be joined to God through Jesus the Christ is the most important decision we will make. It needs to be commemorated and celebrated each year, not by receiving of gifts, but by the giving of gifts. Such gifts are best that build the Kingdom by pouring out ourselves so that others may receive this gift of new life.

Do you remember the date of your baptism or confirmation?

www.ingramcontent.com/pod-product-compliance
Ingram Content Group UK Ltd.
Pitfield, Milton Keynes, MK11 3LW, UK
UKHW041950230426
12048UKWH00008B/242